HEALING THE LAND

Terri Willis

Technical Consultant
Terry Gips
Agricultural Economist
Co-founder/President, International Alliance for
Sustainable Agriculture, Minneapolis, Minnesota

 CHILDRENS PRESS®
CHICAGO

A production of B&B Publishing, Inc.

Editor – Jean Black
Photo Editor – Margie Benson
Computer Specialist – Katy O'Shea

Interior Design – Jean Black/Dave Conant
Artist: Barbara Hammer

Library of Congress Cataloging-in-Publication Data

Willis, Terri
    Healing the Land / by Terri Willis.
        p. cm.
    Includes index.
    ISBN 0-516-05541-0
    1. Environmental degradation -- Juvenile literature. 2. Environmental
education -- Juvenile literature. 3. Environmental policy -- Juvenile literature.
[1. Environmental degradation. 2. Environmental policy] I. Title.
GE140.5.W55 1994
33.73'137--dc20   94-18024
                                                                        CIP
                                                                         AC

Cover photo: Contour-plowed farmland in Wisconsin

Title Page: An environmental engineer examines reclaimed mine land in Wyoming.

Table of Contents page: A manure spreader on a farm in Germany

PHOTO SOURCES

Cover Photo: © B.W. Hoffman
3 M 81; Agripost Inc. 83; American Electric Power 44, 45, 46 both, 52 both, 57, 74 left; American Petroleum Institute 47, 49 right; Arizona State Land Department 13; Dr. Bill Becker 18; California Department of Water Resources 27; © 1988 Robert Caputo/AURORA 5, 6, 9; Chemical Waste Management 79; City of Los Angeles/Ken Meichtry 84 both; City of Orlando 78; Conoco Public Relations 54 both; Dave S. Edwards 24; ©Victor Englebert/Photo Reseachers 56; Environmental Concern Inc. 70 both; FAO photo by C. Bavagnoli 31; FAO photo by F. Mattioli 4; FAO photo by Fiona McDougall 7; FAO photo by I. Pattinson 32; FAO photo by I Velez 23; FAO photo by R. Faidutti 8; Florida Department of Commerce, Division of Tourism 59 right; Terry Gips 3, 38 bottom, 39, 40 top, 41; The Greenway, Denver, Colorado 87 both; GROW 36; Hackensack Meadowlands Development Commission 69; © Michael E. Haritan 51; Carrol Henderson 12 both, 16, 30, 61 bottom, 75; © B.W. Hoffman 37, 42 both; Japan National Tourist Association 76; Kerr McGee 1; Riley N. Kinman, University of Cincinnati 82; © Bob Krist 40 left; Land Stewardship Project 25; Maryland Department of Natural Resources/John Elder 60; Minnesota Board of Water & Soil Resources 22 left; Montana Department of Natural Resources & Conservation 50, 55 both; The Oxford Energy Company 85; © George Holton/Photo Researchers 43; Alison Portello/The Davis Enterprise 86; © Robert Queen 65 both, 74 top; Richard Register 88; Photo courtesy of Saskatchewan Wetland Conservation Corporation 21, 33, 34, 35; © Wolfgang Schuler 28, 29; Soil Conservation Service 10, 80; Soil Science Society of America 14; South Florida Water Management District 62 left; Southern California Edison 53; SURE, Richmond, Indiana 90; Tennessee Valley Authority/Water Quality Department 71, 72; U.S. Fish & Wildlife Service 19 right, 73 right; USDA/Agriculture Research Service 11, 38 top; USDA/Forest Service 19 top, 22 top; USDI/Bureau of Mines 48, 49 bottom, 67; USDI/Bureau of Land Management 20, 26; USDI/FWS, Pennsylvania Field Office 61 top, 62 bottom; John Walters 66; Photo by Michael Wilhelm 58-59; Wisconsin Department of Natural Resources 68, 73 bottom

CONTENTS

Making Changes for the Better

Children who live in the desert village of Korr are always happy to see the camels arrive. The camels are carrying good things to eat from the pastures that lie at a distance from the village. The cattle that graze on the pastures supply the villagers with all the meat and milk they need.

The older children especially are glad to see the supplies. They remember times when there was not enough food for the people or the cattle. The pastures were as dry as deserts. But the villagers worked to improve the land. And they succeeded. Today, the pastures are green and healthy again.

Korr is a tiny village in the Koroli Desert of the East African country of Kenya. Thousands of years ago, there was no desert in that part of Kenya. The land was covered with lush green grass. There were also many lakes and rivers.

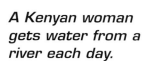

A Kenyan woman gets water from a river each day.

Slowly, over the centuries, weather patterns in the area shifted. Less rain fell, and the landscape changed. Grasses did not grow as well, but other kinds of plants began to appear. Small patches of shrubs and trees took over. Those plants have woody stems and

4

Rendille tribe members and their camels move slowly across the Koroli Desert of Kenya.

Productive wheat and sheep farms cover parts of Kenya.

nomads = people who herd animals and move from place to place to find pasture and good water. They have no fixed home, but depend on their animals for food.

longer roots than grasses do. They can reach down farther into the ground to get water.

The people of the region, called the Rendille, became nomads. They moved about with their cows and goats from one watering hole to the next. They stopped for a while to drink and to eat what foods were available. Once the food and water were gone they moved on. Months or even years passed before the Rendille returned to a particular spot. By then, the plants had grown back, and rain-water had filled the water hole again.

The Rendille lived as nomads for hundreds of years. It was a peaceful way of life. As long as they kept moving, the land provided them with enough to eat and drink.

Tapping into Trouble

About 20 years ago, things changed. The government of Kenya sent workers into the area to drill hundreds of deep holes in the ground. These were wells that could reach the water far below the Earth's surface. The Rendille did not need to move around anymore. Now they simply could draw water from the wells.

Nomads move their sheep and cattle in search of food and water.

Cutting trees for firewood and carrying it home is a daily task for many people around the world.

The government thought the wells would make the lives of the Rendille people better. Instead, the wells caused a disaster.

When the Rendille settled down in one place, they chopped down trees to build houses. Year after year, they chopped down more trees for firewood. Their herds of goats and cattle ate all the grass and shrubs in the area. And they munched right down to the roots of the plants so the vegetation could not grow back.

With no plant roots or trees to hold moist soil in place, the soil dried out and began to blow away. The top layer of the soil contains most of the nutrients, which are substances such as minerals, that plants need to grow. Without this layer, the grass and shrubs could not regrow. The land soon became a desert.

nutrients = the substances in food or fertilizers that allow plants and animals to live and grow.

On the Go Again

It didn't take scientists long to realize that the wells never should have been drilled and that the people never should have been forced to live in one place. In the mid-1980s, people in the government tried to talk the Rendille into moving again.

Their nomadic way of life had kept the land healthy for centuries. The only way to repair the land so that plants could grow once more was for the people to become nomads again.

The Rendille are a happy people who live in harmony with the land.

It was not easy to convince the Rendille people. Many of them liked living in one place. They had no wish to start moving about again. But finally the people agreed at least to move their herds of cattle to pastures farther away. With the cattle eating elsewhere, the pastureland near the village would have a chance to recover.

Today, some Rendille people live in Korr, while others stay with their cattle. The herds are moved often from place to place. Camels travel back and forth between the village and the herds. They carry food and supplies out to the herders. Then the camels return to the village, bringing milk, meat, and skins from the cattle.

The new method is working. The land again supports plant life. And the Rendille people are proud that they are restoring their land.

Problems Around the World

Good land can become desert if people do not use it properly and if weather patterns change.

The Rendille are not the only people facing problems of ruined land. Throughout the world, about one-third of the land is dry and barren. Nothing much grows there.

The amount of desert land in the world is increasing. It is caused by the same destructive things the Rendille did, such as cattle overgrazing the land. Also, people need firewood so they cut down trees. These trees are hard to replace because young trees may be eaten by goats or cut for wood.

Other factors also are causing serious problems for the land. Each year good farmland in North America is blown away by the wind or washed away by heavy rain. In some areas, land is damaged by harmful chemicals. Then people can no longer use it to grow plants. In addition, land is dug up and moved about by mining companies. And people ruin land by building on it or covering it with garbage.

Most of these problems are new to the world. For many centuries, people lived in ways that worked with nature. Like the nomadic life of the Rendille people, their way of life did not harm the land.

This corn field in Georgia gets nutrients from liquid manure, instead of from chemicals.

Today, people are learning new ways to live. New ways can sometimes be good. For example, farmers have learned to grow twice as much food on a field as they once did. We need more food to feed more people. And it's good when miners get materials, such as metals and oil, out of the ground. We need these materials to survive.

We live a better life because of the things we get from the land. But we have to be kind to the land itself. If people do too much damage to the land, there will be no way to grow the food we will need in the future.

Trouble Now

In some parts of Africa, such as Ethiopia, many people already are starving. There are several causes, including improper use of the land. Now the soil cannot support the crops they need for survival.

In other parts of the world, factories are dumping harmful chemicals on the land. Builders are ruining important wetlands. And cities are expanding into farmland, forests, and prairies.

The good news is that we can solve many of these problems. We will see some solutions in later chapters. But first, we must understand why the land is in such danger.

wetlands = lands that are flooded part or all of the year. Many plants and animals live in wetlands.

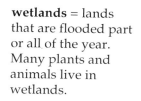

At Hato El Cedral in Venezuela (right), special areas called wetlands on a large cattle ranch have been preserved. Animals such as the giant anteater (above) still find good habitat.

Helping Hands Are Welcome

It takes a lot of garbage to make ten tons (9 metric tons). But some Arizona Boy Scouts cleaned up that much garbage in 1992. They removed all of it from just one piece of land. Their work helped them complete Eagle Scout projects—and it helped the land, too. The projects were led by officials of the Arizona Illegal Dump Fund.

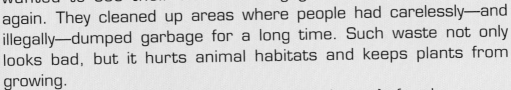

The Illegal Dump Fund is a program of the Environmental Division of the Arizona State Land Department. The fund had only $15,000 to spend in 1992, which isn't much for a government program. Volunteers were needed to get the work done.

Most volunteers were residents who wanted to see their world looking good again. They cleaned up areas where people had carelessly—and illegally—dumped garbage for a long time. Such waste not only looks bad, but it hurts animal habitats and keeps plants from growing.

In 1992, more than 600 tons (540 metric tons) of garbage were cleared from such dumps. And nearly 2,000 old tires were hauled away from spots where thoughtless people had thrown them. The volunteers then disposed of the garbage in the right way.

Many volunteers came from young people's organizations. On one project more than 90 volunteers pitched in for the biggest cleanup of the year. They borrowed equipment and trucks to remove 295 tons (268 metric tons) of garbage and 800 old tires that had been dumped illegally on one piece of land.

Getting Down to the Ground

Seeds are planted in the top layer of the soil called top-soil (above).

topsoil = the surface layer of soil in which most of the nutrients are found.

Most of us never thought we'd have to worry about losing our land. After all, there's so much of it. When we dig a hole and take away a pailful of dirt, there is always more soil underneath.

The problem is that we are losing a certain kind of land. We are losing and polluting some of the best soil on Earth for growing food and the best land for wild animals and plants. And this land is very important for people, too.

What makes this land so special? Well, the upper layer of ground—called topsoil—contains many nutrients that help plants grow. Almost all plants depend on topsoil, whether they are growing in a garden, in a forest, on a prairie, or on a farm. And animals depend on the plants.

Topsoil is one of the most important natural resources in the world. A natural resource is anything in or on the Earth that people can use.

There are two kinds of resources, renewable and nonrenewable. Renewable resources can be replaced. Nonrenewable resources are used once and then are gone forever. Trees are a renewable resource. We plant more trees to replace those we cut down. Coal is a nonrenewable resource. Once we burn it up, it takes centuries for more to form.

natural resource = a material found in or on the Earth that is useful to people.

Terrific Topsoil

Topsoil is considered a nonrenewable resource. Though nature can form more topsoil, it takes thousands of years.

Trees are a renewable resource, but it takes years to wait for them to grow.

A black witch moth rests on a rock that has patches of orange lichen.

Topsoil usually starts off as rocks. Over many centuries, the rocks are broken up into tiny particles. This happens in many ways. Heavy rains wash down on them, carrying particles away. Wind blows small stones over them, chipping off pieces. Some chemicals in the air, or ice that gets in cracks, make stones break apart. Even some small plants, called lichens, can do this. Lichens grow on rocks. They contain chemicals that cause rocks to break up slowly into tiny pieces.

There are living things in topsoil too. When you scoop up a handful of soil from your garden, it seems dead and lifeless. But it contains millions of plants and creatures so small that they are hard to see. There are microorganisms, tiny insects, and even tiny animals in a handful of soil.

lichen = a combination of two plants—a one-celled plant called an alga and a fungus.

microorganism = an animal or plant such as bacteria or fungus, that is so small it can be seen only with a microscope (right).

Microorganisms are so small they can't be seen without a microscope, but they do a big job. They digest leaves and the remains of dead plants and animals. This process breaks down the remains, or decomposes them, into the nutrients that built them in the first place.

The part of the topsoil containing decomposed material from living things is called humus. The main nutrients that humus adds to the soil are carbon, nitrogen, and sulfur.

A variety of small creatures are found in topsoil. There may be adult insects or young insects called larvae, such as maggots. Earthworms and many-legged centipedes are usually found in good topsoil. Like microorganisms, they help turn dead plants and animals into nutrients. Animals do this by feeding on dead material, living plants, insects, and even animal waste. Their bodies digest the material. It returns to the soil as nutrients in their excrement, or waste. These creatures also make holes in the soil, which allows air and water to enter.

The things that live and grow in the soil are part of a cycle—a pattern that is repeated over and over. First, the plants use nutrients from the soil to grow. Then, when the plants die, they fall to the ground, returning plant material to the soil. Or an animal eats the plant, digests it, and returns plant material to the soil in its excrement. The microorganisms

decompose = to break down into nutrients that can be re-used by plants and animals.

humus = the richest part of soil containing nutrients from decomposed plant and animal matter.

Centipede

Earthworm

Earthworm Magic

The farm fields of Illinois produce much of the corn and soybeans in the United States. But most farmers use chemical fertilizers to get good crops. When Dr. Bill Becker studied the soil in the state, he found that the soil in many fields no longer contained earthworms.

But there was one farmer whose fields had many earthworms. This farmer grew lots of crops, but he used no chemical fertilizers. Instead, he depended on worms to break down the organic material and add nutrients to the soil.

He kept the worms in his fields by doing less plowing. When tractors pass over a field, they pack down the soil too much while plows turn it upside down. This destroys the worm's habitat.

But in fields where there is a minimum of plowing, and no chemical fertilizers are added, worms can grow and multiply. They

feed on dead or decaying material, such as plants left behind in the field. They digest this food, and their waste helps create humus. Humus puts nutrients back into the soil.

Presently, Dr. Becker teaches people about the benefits of earthworms. He helps farmers learn how to keep these wonderful creatures in their soil.

The forest floor is covered with decomposing leaves, plants, and trees (left). Animals, such as muskrats (below), eat plants and pass the remains in their excrement.

and small animals in the soil then go to work on the plant materials, breaking them down into nutrients. New plants use the nutrients as they grow. And the cycle continues year after year.

Harming the Land

Unfortunately, we do many things that break this natural cycle. The cycle is broken when people harm, or misuse, the land. But we now recognize how serious this harm can be.

It has taken a long time for people to see the problems with the land. Land problems often develop slowly, over many years. And people don't notice the damage being done until it is too late.

Think of the wind blowing over a beach. Each gust of wind picks up a few grains of sand and blows them away. A few grains make very little difference. But what happens when this goes on day and night for many years? Eventually, the beach is gone. It has been carried off by the wind.

Sometimes recreational vehicles tear up the soil and the wind carries it away.

erosion = the wearing away of land surfaces by the action of wind or water.

This is called erosion, and it is a real problem. It doesn't happen just on beaches either. Precious soil also is being carried away from farm fields, wilderness areas, construction sites, and many other places.

Wind Carries Soil Away

Wind erosion occurs most often in places where there are no growing plants. A farm field often has no plants after the crops have been harvested. Construction sites are bare where the ground has been torn up, and so are beaches. Wind erosion can harm the land at such places. When rainfall is sparse and soil is dry, wind can easily pick it up.

Sometimes the wind picks up very small pieces of soil, and carries them long distances. These tiny dry particles of eroded soil can hang in the air like dust. They make life very difficult for people with breathing problems. Other times, larger pieces of soil roll along the ground, pushed by the wind.

In the United States and Canada, wind erosion on farm fields is a big problem. About one inch (2.5 centimeters) of topsoil is lost every 30 years. That may not seem like a lot, but it took more than 500 years for just an inch of topsoil to develop. The problem is even greater in countries where the land does not have enough humus to keep it moist.

Topsoil is lost from farm fields when the wind blows and there are no crops to hold the soil in place.

Water Washes Soil Away

Water also can cause erosion in several ways. When raindrops land on the ground, the drops can

This farmland in Mississippi has been badly eroded by running water.

Some builders put up fences so soil won't wash away when it rains.

carry soil with them as they flow downhill. Sometimes the rain carves small channels in the ground. Water flowing down these channels carries more soil with it. Very heavy rains can form deep channels called gullies. Gullies carry away even more water and soil. As the water flow increases, the gullies get wider and deeper.

Water erosion is common in empty farm fields where there are no crops to hold the soil in place. Water erosion also is becoming more common in cities. Most city land is covered with buildings, parking lots, and streets. Since rainwater can't soak into concrete or hardened ground, most of it runs downhill across the surface. When it hits the softer soil found in ditches and on hills, it can cause erosion. It also can cause flooding in low areas because the water has no place to go and cannot soak in to already saturated ground.

In the End

Where does all the topsoil go after it has been carried away by wind and water erosion? It builds up in places where it is not wanted. Then it is called sediment.

Sediment builds up in ditches and gutters, as well as along railroads, fences, and buildings. Cleaning sediment out of these areas can be costly.

Sediment often settles in streams, rivers, and lakes where it slows the flow of water. It covers up the places where fish lay their eggs and where waterbirds feed. Some sediment flows into the ocean, damaging harbors. It can block the passage of ships and boats.

The best way to stop erosion is to grow trees and plants. The roots help hold the soil in place. Plants also keep raindrops from striking soil too hard. Land covered with trees and plants does not erode easily.

But some pieces of land, such as deserts and some beaches, grow only a few plants. This land lacks the nutrients and moisture plants need. After harvesting, some farm fields do not have plants either. We need to find ways to keep the soil in such places from being eroded.

This man in Peru plants eucalyptus trees to stop erosion on a hillside.

Pollution

Another problem is pollution. We pollute our land, water, and air when we add a harmful substance that doesn't belong there. Pollution can be very dangerous. Poisonous chemicals can get into a river and kill all the fish. Or smoke pumped up by tall chimneys can poison the air. Water and air can be polluted, and so can land.

Land is polluted when harmful chemicals get into the ground. They can make it impossible for plants to grow. Usually, these chemicals are used in making products that we use or eat. The chemicals come from factories, gas stations, farms, and homes. More than 70,000 chemicals are used in homes and businesses every day—and some of them are harmful.

We are trying to stop using harmful chemicals and trying to find safe alternatives. In the meantime, people who work with these chemicals must be very careful, especially when they dispose of them.

Usually, harmful chemicals are kept out of the soil. Sometimes accidents happen, but other times people are careless or lazy. They throw harmful chemicals onto the ground, rather than get rid of them in the right way. For example, some people pour used oil from their cars onto the ground. They don't want to carry it to gas stations where there are special tanks for dumping used oil.

Sometimes people dump barrels of harmful waste in forests.

Children Win the Battle

Nearly 1,000 children picked up shovels and went to work planting trees. They were fighting erosion on the steep hillsides along the Mississippi River near Winona, Minnesota.

The children were volunteers in a program run by the Land Stewardship Project based in Lewiston, Minnesota. This project is designed to help preserve soil and water resources throughout the Midwest.

One of the main goals of the project is to teach children about taking care of the planet. The first step is giving children an active role in caring for the land. People who see themselves as a part of the Earth hopefully will lead others in the fight to save our resources.

Erosion wasn't always a problem in Winona. Before settlers came to the area, the hills were covered with trees and shrubs. But when settlers arrived in the early 1800s, they wanted to farm. They cut down the trees to make room for growing crops and raising cattle. With the plants gone, much of the topsoil slid into the valley and was washed away by the Mississippi.

By 1992, the children had planted more than 23,000 trees. The trees' roots grew deep into the ground. They help to hold the soil in place, even during heavy rains. It was a battle against erosion, and the children won!

No matter how chemicals enter the land, they can cause problems for a long time. Some chemicals cause damage for thousands of years! Most pollution can be cleaned up, but it is very expensive and hard to get all of it.

Good Land Gone Bad

desertification = a process in which good, healthy land is turned into desert. Harmful farming practices may cause desertification.

Another problem that the land faces is desertification. This happens when healthy land is damaged so badly that it becomes useless for growing things.

When the land is misused year after year, it can become so badly damaged that nothing grows on it. Overgrazing (putting too many cattle on the land) and other activities can make the soil useless.

Sometimes the weather patterns change in an area and the land dries out slowly over many years. Most of the world's deserts were formed in this way, like the area around Korr in Kenya.

Sometimes desertification occurs because people have harmed the land. When the land is damaged so that no plants can grow, erosion occurs. Or ranchers may let too many animals graze on a piece of land. Then the animals eat the plants all the way down to the roots and the plants cannot regrow. Soon wind and rain carry away the topsoil. Pollution also makes it difficult for plants to grow.

Sometimes cattle eat plants down to the ground, exposing the topsoil.

Desertification is taking place all around the world. Some experts say that the process could destroy more than one-third of the world's land if people don't do something about it quickly.

Fortunately, there are ways to help solve these problems. We must all work to save the land and its precious topsoil. We need to be able to grow enough food for people now and in the future. We need to allow wildlife to live. And we want to keep our world beautiful.

We need to keep our soil healthy so farmers can grow enough food to feed the Earth's people.

Farming for the Future

This Aymara family in Peru grows potatoes using ancient methods (above).

If you were to fly low in a small plane over the western border of Bolivia in South America, you would notice something interesting. Down below, you'd see a criss-cross pattern of canals filled with water. Between the canals lie raised plots of ground covered with lush green plants. You would be looking at an ancient method of growing plants that people have started using again.

This special place is near the town of Tiwanaku, on the shore of Lake Titicaca. Lake Titicaca, the highest big lake in the world, is located at an elevation of more than 12,000 feet (3,650 meters). It gets very cold at that elevation.

Until a few years ago, the Aymara people who farmed the land were having problems. Often, cold air killed the crops. Also, potatoes often rotted in the ground because the soil was too wet all the time. The people were able to raise very little food on that land.

In 1987 the Aymara learned from American researchers that their land once had provided plenty of food. More than 1,000 years ago, the Indians that farmed the land dug canals and planted on the high ground between the canals. It worked well for hundreds of years. The Americans encouraged the people to try this "canal farming" again. Most people didn't think it would work, but one man decided to try canal farming. He dug the canals and he planted on the high ground. His neighbors thought he was crazy. But his plants grew better than theirs did that year. The secret was that the water in the canals formed a mist over his plants at night. The mist protected the plants from the cold air. And the raised planting areas let water drain from the soil so his potatoes didn't rot.

When others saw how well canal farming worked, they also dug canals and began planting on the high ground. Now the Aymara grow all the food they need. These farmers have learned how to make the best use of their land.

Aymara potato harvests increased when the people began using the farming methods of their ancestors.

Food from Soil

Land and soil are important to people. Most fruits, vegetables, and grains grow in soil. Animals need grains and grasses from the land to give us meat, milk, eggs, wool, and many other products.

In some parts of the world, people still go into the wilderness to gather food. These gatherers are mostly native people who live everywhere from the rain forests of South America to the plains of Africa and Australia. However, nearly everyone else in the world depends on farmers to provide their food.

developing countries = countries where the industry and economy are not modern.

Like the Aymara people, some farmers in developing countries use old basic methods to work the soil. They use simple tools or plows pulled by oxen, horses, or other animals. They generally produce just enough food for their own families.

In other parts of the world, huge tractors move swiftly across the land. They pull machines that

This farmer in Venezuela prepares his soil with a simple plow pulled by oxen.

prepare the soil, plant seeds, add nutrients, or harvest crops. Some farmers grow enough to feed hundreds of people.

But whether farmers use simple tools or enormous machines, they all want the same result—good crops and healthy land.

When farmland is cared for, it usually remains fertile—plants are able to grow on it. Throughout history, farmers used several methods to keep the land fertile.

Farmers in Togo plant yams in high dirt mounds that protect their crops from flooding and keep the soil loose.

fertile = having enough nutrients to grow crops.

Giving Back to the Land

Some farmers kept their land fertile by plowing plant remains, such as corn stalks, leaves, and roots, back into the land. The remains of such crops as corn and beans, plus animal manure, added the necessary nutrients. Other farmers planted one type of crop one year, and another type of crop the next year.

Some farmers preserved cropland by terracing hillsides. They carved large steps into a hillside and planted on the flat tops of the steps. This works better than planting on the slope of the hill, because it keeps the soil from washing away in heavy rains.

Beautiful vegetable gardens are often planted on terraced hillsides in the highlands of Malaysia.

One of the best things farmers did for their land was to let it lie fallow—or unplanted—every other year. This allows the land to rest and gives tiny creatures time to build up the soil's nutrients again.

But as the world's population grew, farmers needed to grow even more food. The farmers' methods changed to meet this need.

More Food, More Problems

Unfortunately, some of the things that help farmers grow more food also harm soil. In the last few decades, much topsoil from around the world has been lost, mostly due to poor agriculture practices and cutting down forests.

It is hard for farmers to let land lie fallow for a year when they could plant crops on it instead. People want the food that can be grown on this land and farmers need money. Unfortunately, the soil then loses nutrients that are not replaced.

Also, farmers often plant many fields with the same crop year after year. This drains important nutrients from the soil and puts it out of balance.

In order to replace the nutrients that are lost, some farmers add chemical fertilizers. These chemicals are sprayed on the land using large machines. These fertilizers are meant to replace nutrients that once were provided by plant and animal decomposition. They help plants grow. But they are expensive and can kill earthworms and other soil organisms that provide natural nutrients. When it rains, fertilizers can run off farmland into lakes and streams where they cause pollution.

Many farmers also apply pesticides to their fields. These chemicals keep out weeds, prevent fungus from growing on plants, and are used to kill insects that eat up crops. Pesticides can help farmers produce bigger crops, but they are expen-

This farm field is "resting" between crops. The farmer has planted clover and alfalfa that will put nutrients back into the soil.

fertilizer = a substance applied to soil to add nutrients.

pesticide = a chemical used to kill weeds, fungi, insects, or rodents.

33

When farmers let crop stubble decompose in the soil, it fertilizes the ground. Stubble is also a good place for ducks to nest.

tilling = plowing the land to prepare it for raising crops.

sive and they can harm our air, water, and food. Finally, when the same type of pesticide is used year after year, some pests build up a resistance to it. The pesticide no longer kills the insects and weeds. Farmers then have to apply a different kind of chemical—and use even more of it.

American farmers use about 19 million tons (17 million metric tons) of chemical fertilizers and a quarter of a million tons (113,400 kilograms) of pesticides on their fields every year. After several years, fertilizers and pesticides build up in the soil and often plants will not grow there.

Tilling for Trouble

Still more problems are caused by tilling. Farmers till the land to prepare it for planting. They plow through the soil to loosen it. But when it is loose, topsoil is easily blown or washed away.

Throughout the world, farmers are losing about 24 billion tons (21.8 billion metric tons) of topsoil every year. In the United States alone, more than 1.5 billion tons (1.4 billion metric tons) are lost annually. America has lost at least one-third of all its topsoil in the past 200 years.

Most of this loss has occurred in the last 50 years. Farmers have used new ways to grow more food, and that is important. But now we're learning how harmful some of these new methods are.

Today, many farmers are trying other ways—some new and some old—to grow food and protect the land at the same time.

A Sustainable Solution

Many of these other methods fall under the heading of "sustainable agriculture." Sustainable agriculture is any way of farming that keeps the soil and environment healthy for the future, while still growing enough food to feed people today.

Sustainable agriculture does not involve one specific method. What works in one part of the world does not always work in other places. Each farmer must select what works best for him or her.

sustainable agriculture = growing enough healthy food for everyone in a way that won't hurt the Earth or its people.

Here, farmers in Canada plant their seeds directly on the stubble from the last year. Topsoil won't erode as easily when using this method.

The Aymara people, for example, used a type of sustainable agriculture when they planted between the canals. That canal method wouldn't be useful in many other places. But there are a few common sustainable agriculture practices that many farmers use.

SUCCESS STORY

GROW a Garden

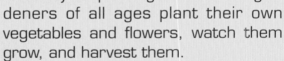

The city of Washington, D.C. has some tough neighborhoods. But now people in these areas are having fun among bright patches of green. They get together to plant gardens on vacant lots.

The gardens are community gardens. Several people care for small patches of land on each lot. Garden Resources of Washington (GROW) watches these gardens and offers help.

Planting gardens on vacant lots is a good way to make use of land that would otherwise go to waste. People who live in the neighborhood must first clean up all the trash on the lot. GROW teaches them how to get the soil ready for planting. Then these gardeners of all ages plant their own vegetables and flowers, watch them grow, and harvest them.

Gardens have been started in back alleys, in public housing yards, and on church property. They add a touch of beauty to crowded neighborhoods. They grow food for families. And they bring people together to use land in a way that is good for the environment and the community.

The Olden Days Had Better Ways

Some of these "new" farming methods are much like the methods farmers used long ago. For example, many farmers apply animal manure to their fields. They also leave behind the plant waste from crops in the field to decompose. Both the manure and the plants put nutrients back into the soil.

Another old-time practice is multiple crop rotation. Farmers plant several types of crops, such as soybeans, corn, and wheat, and grow them in different fields each season. In this way, the same crop is not taking the same nutrients out of a field year after year.

Instead of tilling their fields, some farmers are trying no-till. They drop seed on the ground right on top of the plant residue of the previous year. These crops can grow well while the rich topsoil remains in place. The moisture stays in the ground, too. This helps feed the plants.

Some farmers who have hilly land plant in curving rows along the hills, rather than in straight lines. This is called contour cropping. The rows are planted across the hill instead of downhill. Rainwater cannot flow down easily between the plants so the soil does not wash away.

Farmers plow hillsides along the curves, or contours, to stop soil from eroding.

Getting Bugged by Bugs

Bugs are another problem that sustainable agriculture can help deal with. Some insects eat plants

Diamondback moth larvae are pests that eat cabbage, cauliflower, and broccoli plants.

and cause other damage. Often, farmers use certain pesticides, called insecticides, to fight insects. But insecticides can poison the soil. So, many farmers are trying something different. They are using helpful or beneficial insects to fight harmful ones.

Cabbage worms are larvae, much like caterpillars, before they become butterflies. As larvae, they burrow into and eat vegetables such as broccoli and cabbage. Before they turn into butterflies, these worms can damage crops.

Farmers often spray insecticides to get rid of the larvae. But today, some farmers release certain types of wasps and flies into their fields. These "good" insects lay their eggs on the larvae. When the eggs hatch, the new insects eat the larvae. The helpful insects are not harmful to the land, to crops, or to human health. They do the same job as pesticides but without poisoning the land, and they cost much less.

This farmer in Israel raises a kind of wasp that doesn't hurt people. These wasps are released in the fields where they lay eggs on other pests, killing them.

In Michigan, researchers fenced an apple orchard and put in chickens. They wanted to see if chickens would be a natural way to stop the many insects that can harm apple trees. They got a pleasant surprise when they learned that the chickens did two useful things. They not only ate the insects, but they also kept weeds from growing in the orchard by walking on them and eating them.

Some farmers in Israel place containers in their fields that give off a scent to attract insect pests. The pests are lured inside the container where they die. Pesticides are not needed.

Nature even provides many of these insect controls naturally. For example, spiders catch a range of harmful pests in their webs. Birds eat huge numbers of insects as part of their diet. Indeed, we can work with nature and avoid dangerous pesticides, whether at home, in the garden, or on the farm.

Will We Go Hungry?

Sustainable agriculture obviously is good for the soil. But we also need to ask: Can farmers make a

Food grown without chemicals can look as beautiful as food grown with chemicals (right), and it is often more nutritious (below).

living and also grow enough food to feed everyone?

Scientists don't agree on the answer. Some say that if farmers gave up all pesticides and chemical fertilizers, it would be a disaster. They point out that while farmers used to grow food without fertilizers, there were not as many people to feed back then.

Other experts say that farmers should give up chemical fertilizers and pesticides slowly. That way, they can learn new sustainable agriculture methods as they go along. They will find out what works best for them—and they can still use chemicals if necessary.

Another group of researchers believes farmers have to quit using chemical fertilizers and pesticides immediately. They agree that some farmers might produce less, but say that most farmers would save money and everyone would still get enough food. Not only would the food be of higher quality and safer, but we wouldn't have to pay for cleaning up the soil and water in the future.

At present we have huge storehouses of extra food, but some people are starving. We can't always get the food to people who need it. Experts believe that people in developing nations must have the education and resources to grow their own food so they don't have to depend on others. Sustainable agriculture could help them, too.

Saving Soil Without Starvation

In the African nation of Burkina Faso, some farmers are using a very simple sustainable method. They put rows of stones across hillsides in their fields. When it rains, water can't wash soil down the hill. Instead, the water sinks slowly into the soil and helps plants grow.

This farmer in Burkina Faso built simple erosion control lines to stop rain from washing away the precious topsoil.

Where farmers have used this simple method, they have produced more crops. At present much of the land in Burkina Faso is not fit for growing crops. But if more farmers use the rows of stones, experts say that the soil could become good for planting once again.

Some North American farmers also are finding that they can grow as much food using sustainable agriculture as they did using fertilizers and pesticides. Glen and Rex Spray of Ohio have used sustainable agriculture

The use of chemical fertilizers can be reduced by planting different crops in rows and alternating them in different years (below). Planting different crops side by side can help control pests (inset).

methods on their land for 15 years. In that time they have used no chemical fertilizers or pesticides. Instead, they spread manure from their cows onto the fields to add nutrients. Each year they rotate their crops of corn, beans, and small grains into different fields to keep down insects and disease. It all works. They produce greater yields, or amounts, on their fields than other area farmers.

The Sprays are not the only farmers doing well with sustainable agriculture. Everywhere farmers are finding that it is a good way to grow the food we need, while keeping soil healthy for the future.

Take Back the Land

The Shipibo people of Peru have lived in the forests along Peru's Amazon River for centuries. But in the mid-1960s a major road was built through their land. Outsiders moved in and began to cut down trees. They began to use the land for farming and grazing cattle.

But the land was not suited for these purposes. Plants didn't grow well on the land so chemical fertilizers were used. Within 20 years, the land was almost useless. Many farms were abandoned.

But the Shipibo had a plan to repair their land. With help from their government, they leased a small, abandoned pasture and planted crops on it. They used sustainable agriculture methods. Within five years, the soil was rich once again. They grew more crops than other nearby farms that used chemical fertilizers.

How did the Shipibo people do it? First, they created raised planting areas, with ditches between them. The ditches stored rainwater so there always was enough moisture in the soil.

They added leaves and animal waste to the planting areas to add nutrients to the soil. They kept out insect pests by growing plants that pests dislike, such as marigolds and sesame.

The Shipibo also noticed that many different plants grow together in the forest. They began growing more than 40 types of plants together, along with fruit trees.

The Shipibo people plan to take over more of the damaged land. They want to make it useful again. Today, they are teaching their sustainable agriculture methods throughout Peru.

Problems Are Yours and "Mine"

There is a place in southeastern Ohio with trees as far as you can see. Peaceful hills and valleys are dotted with lakes and ponds. Many animals make their homes here, and people are welcome to enjoy it all.

It is a lovely place, but it is unusual too. Less than 50 years ago, the area looked very different. It was an abandoned coal mine. Much of the soil had been dug up and taken away. Nothing grew there. However, people didn't like seeing the wasteland. They worked hard to make changes. Today, it is a 30,000-acre (12,000-hectare) special place called ReCreation Land.

Hundreds of thousands of people now come to ReCreation Land each year. They camp, hike, boat, and fish. Most agree that the scenery looks wonderful. It's hard to believe that heavy machines roared across the landscape not long ago. The machines dug up the ground to get to the coal that lay beneath it. Now, beavers, deer, owls, geese, groundhogs, foxes, and raccoons live on the land. In the lakes, bluegills, bass, catfish, sunfish, northern pike, and crappies thrive.

Geese and many other animals (below) now live in Ohio's ReCreation Land. Fishing is a favorite pastime in this area (opposite).

When land is reclaimed, topsoil is spread to cover gently rolling hills (right). Then, grass seed is planted. Organic material called mulch that will hold the seed in place is distributed on land that has been planted (below).

Coal Was the Goal

In the mid-1940s, the Ohio Power Company began mining coal in southeastern Ohio. Before that time, the land had been used for agriculture. But the soil was poor, and the farmers didn't make much money. Ohio Power came in and stripped away layers of topsoil and clay. Big machines dug down deep to get to the coal. Some of it lay 180 feet (54 meters) below the surface of the Earth.

After the miners got all the coal, they could have left the ugly mess. Instead, they replaced the soil, forming hills and valleys. They created lakes and ponds.

Some of the land was planted with trees and shrubs. These plants grew into thick forests of pine, cottonwood, maple, ash, oak, and more. In other places, new grasses were planted to cover gentle hills, creating pastureland. The hills and ponds were planned carefully to prevent soil erosion and provide habitat for wildlife.

Today, more than three million tons (2.7 million metric tons) of coal still are mined each year from the region around ReCreation Land. This coal provides electricity for about eight million people in seven states. And as this valuable resource is taken from the ground, the mining company continues to repair the surrounding area.

Energy from Coal

Coal mining in North America began more than 200 years ago. Coal is a mineral that can be burned to power mechanical things, such as train engines and machines in factories. For a long time, people used coal to heat their homes in

Coal is often transported in long trains.

winter. Today, in many places, coal is burned to create electricity.

But coal lies underground, where it formed over millions of years. In order to get to it, mining companies have to tear open the land. They use large machines to break up the coal and dig it out. In the past, when they had taken all the coal, the mining companies simply moved on, leaving a ruined landscape behind.

This happened all over the world. Coal mining left many deep scars on the Earth, where there was once beautiful wilderness.

Mining for Our Lives

Mining companies take many elements people need from the ground. Bikes are made from metals that have been mined, and so are copper kettles, aluminum soda cans, and skyscrapers. Ingredients in cement come from mining, and so do some of the ingredients in fertilizers that help grow our food. Without the products we get from mining, our lives would be very different.

There are several ways to get to these minerals. One method is called open-pit mining. Huge holes are dug into the land, so that big machines can scoop out the minerals. An iron-ore mine in Hibbing, Minnesota, is the largest man-made hole on Earth. It is visible from outer space.

Tunnel mining is another way to reach the minerals, especially those, like coal that lie deep

Coal and other minerals are often mined far below the surface. This huge equipment is moving valuable minerals through a large underground opening during mining operations.

beneath the Earth's surface. Miners ride an elevator down a shaft dug into the ground. They arrive at tunnels that have been carved out far below the surface. The miners remove minerals from the tunnel walls and send them back to the Earth's surface on little trains.

Another way to get coal is by strip mining, sometimes called surface mining. This type of mining gets its name from the long strips of land that are dug up and piled alongside the trench. Machines scoop out the minerals that have been uncovered, and put the remaining land back in place. This is the cheapest and safest way to mine coal and many other minerals.

Chemical mining is often used to obtain ore—

Huge shovels (left) scoop coal from the ground. It takes a giant boom or counterweight, like the one shown above, to balance a huge shovel as it does its work. This boom is 27 feet (8 meters) tall.

Tailings, or waste, from a gold and silver mine in Montana scar the land.

tailings = the waste material left after a mineral is separated from rocks.

small amounts of minerals found in rocks. For example, tiny grains of gold sometimes can be found in the rocky sides of mountains. Mining companies spray the mountainsides with chemicals that break up the rock and release the gold. The rock slides down the mountain, and the gold is sifted out.

Iron is another mineral that is separated from ore by chemicals. The leftover rock is called tailings. Sometimes the tailings and the chemicals are left behind, causing pollution. Cyanide, a chemical often used in mining, can poison fish and animals. Mining companies must remove the harmful chemicals when they clean up the land.

Making over the Mines

Usually, land can be cleaned up and the mining scars healed through a process called land reclamation. Reclamation can repair the land so that it can be used again. In some countries large areas have been left scarred and not reclaimed because the process is too expensive. In the United States, most reclamation projects now take place during the mining process. Reclamation also protects water and soil resources around the mines.

There are many uses for reclaimed land. Some reclaimed land is used for agriculture. If an area had poor soil, mining companies might replace it with soil good for growing crops. Or grass can be planted, and the land used for grazing animals. Mining companies sometimes create lakes when they reclaim land. If they dig large holes deep enough, rainwater will form lakes in the holes. The new lakes help the animals in the area. Vacation resorts with golf courses can be built on such land.

reclamation = the process of repairing damaged land, so that it can be used for farmland, recreation, or other useful purposes.

This reclaimed mining land in Pennsylvania is now an outdoor theater.

An American Electric Power employee inspects the grass cover at this reclaimed mine site in West Virginia (right). The soil was mixed with fly ash and several other nutrients so trees and grass could grow (below).

Or reclaimed land may be left to grow whatever will grow, which may be somewhat different.

From Bare to Beautiful

A few years ago, West Virginia had a large area that was black and bare. The waste from an old coal mine was all that could be seen. But today, the land has turned green with grass, shrubs, and young trees.

American Electric Power owned the coal mine and was required by law to repair the site. But they had a problem. The mining waste on top of the land was not good for growing plants. The company found an interesting way to solve their problem.

They owned a nearby power plant that produced a waste product, called fly ash, when coal was burned in the big furnaces. They mixed the fly ash with the mining waste, along with several nutrients. This made the soil right for growing plants. Now healthy plants cover the old mine.

Bring Back the Beauty

The Sierra National Forest near North Fork, California, is a popular spot for people who enjoy the outdoors. Visitors hike, hunt, and fish in the beautiful wilderness. However, many people noticed some really ugly spots on their hikes through the forest.

In the late 1950s, a tunnel had been dug in the area by the California Edison Company as part of an electric power project. Drilling and blasting through rock created a great deal of waste that was dumped in a large pit and buried. But then erosion carried away the soil cover, so the ugly and dangerous waste lay out in the open. Few plants grew in the area, and erosion threatened to carry away much of the nearby hillside.

In 1991, California Edison decided to clean up the mess and restore the area. First, workers removed most of the debris. Then they added soil and planted grasses and trees on the land. The plants made the area look prettier and stopped further erosion by holding the soil in place. They attracted wildlife, too.

While working on this project, California Edison learned many good ways to restore a waste site. Now, they share this information with people who want to clean up areas near power projects, gold mines, and construction sites.

A Cleanup in Texas

Another sort of reclamation project took place as part of the Conquista Project, a South Texas uranium mining operation in five counties. Uranium is a valuable mineral used in making nuclear energy. The company in charge was Conoco. Reclamation began while the mining work was going on.

Reclaiming the tailings pond and the land around it was a major task. It had to be done carefully, because uranium tailings contain harmful chemicals.

Conoco first buried the dangerous tailings under many feet of soil. Then they covered the soil with hard-packed clay to keep rainwater from seeping down into the wastes. On top they put good topsoil.

Experts helped decide what plants would be best for the area. They chose several grasses that grow quickly and have strong roots. The roots help hold the topsoil in place during strong winds and heavy rains. Now, the pollutants are locked far below the Earth's surface and, on top, beautiful grasses blow in the breeze.

Uranium tailings were buried during the Conquista Project (top). Today this same area is a grassy prairie with a water reservoir full of fish (bottom).

Superfund Is Not Super Fun

Unfortunately, not all mines are properly reclaimed. In the United States, for example, about 50 old mines are now Superfund sites. Companies that pollute must pay large amounts of money into a cleanup fund, Superfund, formed by the government. Each cleanup site will cost millions of dollars to reclaim, and the process will take years.

An abandoned copper mine—the Berkeley Mine in Montana— is the largest Superfund site. Thousands of acres of land around the mine have been polluted, and harmful chemicals have seeped down into the groundwater. About 130 miles (209 kilometers) of riverways also have been polluted. People are working to improve the Berkeley Mine, but the pollution is so widespread that they won't be able to clean all of it.

Developing countries often have serious pollution from mining because there are no controls in place. The pollution is especially bad in areas where industry is growing rapidly, such as regions of East Asia. South America, particularly in the

groundwater = water that fills the spaces found in some rock formations beneath the Earth's surface. Groundwater often is used for drinking water by digging a well down into it.

The huge hole left from the Berkeley Mine in Montana is filling with polluted water (far left). Plans are being made to clean up this old mine. Other mining regions already been have successfully reclaimed in Montana (left).

Andes Mountains, also suffers from heavy pollution caused by mining.

Losing a Lifestyle

Sometimes, it's not only land that is harmed by mining. Human beings and their entire way of life can be threatened. In the Amazon region of Brazil, a group of native people called the Yanomami live as their ancestors had lived for centuries. Nature provides them with all they need for their food, clothing, and homes.

This boy belongs to the Yanomami tribe of people who live on land protected by the government of Brazil.

The Yanomami faced serious problems when thousands of miners came to their homeland in search of gold and other valuable minerals. The miners tore up their land and polluted their rivers. The Yanomami people found it difficult to get the food they needed to survive.

At first, the leaders of Brazil refused to stop the mining companies. They thought it was more important to get the minerals from the land, so the country could make money. But eventually, they changed their minds and decided to help the native Yanomami people. In 1991, a large reserve, where mining was banned, was created for the Yanomami.

Mining and Money

More and more countries are passing laws to help stop the problems caused by mining. But such choices can be difficult in the world's developing countries.

Developing countries want good roads, sturdy buildings, and productive factories. These countries need such things to improve the lives of their people. But mining is necessary to get the materials needed for roads, buildings, and factories. Governments must decide whether to help the country get wealthier or save the land.

It is possible to do both, but it will take good planning and great effort. In Chile, a mining company is flushing water through the waste material from a copper mine to remove copper that used to be left behind. This project saves money and keeps waste out of a local river, so there will be less pollution.

When land is reclaimed it may not look exactly as it did before, but it can be made very beautiful and useful.

Mining is important. We could not live the way we do without mining. Reclamation is a good way to use the Earth's minerals and still help the environment. Of course, land that has been reclaimed isn't exactly the way it was before it was mined. People can never copy nature perfectly. But it's important to keep trying.

Wetlands such as this one in Oregon (above), owned by the Wetlands Conservancy, are places for people to enjoy nature.

Wonderful Wetlands

There are several special places in Oregon where people enjoy a quiet moment. Visitors can bring a picnic lunch. They can sit quietly and watch birds and wildlife. They can hike on trails and learn more about the plants and animals that live in this area.

These special places are wetlands owned by the Wetlands Conservancy in Oregon. Wetlands are areas that hold water at least part of each year. The conservancy is an organization formed to protect these natural resources.

The Wetlands Conservancy was formed in 1981

to raise money to protect wetlands. The group buys wetlands that otherwise would be destroyed by pollution or new buildings. It owns more than 60 acres (24 hectares) of wetlands. The wetlands are used for wildlife, research, and education. And visitors are welcome to visit. The conservancy helps people learn more about wetlands and their importance, so that everyone will help preserve these natural treasures.

Beautiful water-birds such as egrets live in some wetlands.

Many people think that wetlands are not important. People can't grow food on them or build houses on them. But wetlands are important in the balance of nature.

More plants and animals can live and grow in

one acre (0.4 hectare) of certain kinds of wetlands than in the same area of forest or anywhere else. This is true because the water in wetlands is usually quite shallow, perhaps less than six feet (1.8 meters) deep. Thus, sun can shine through the water and help the plants grow. The shallow water also warms quickly, so plants in wetlands have a longer growing season than other plants.

Ducks often rest in wetland areas when they migrate north and south each year. The wetlands shown here are located along Maryland's shoreline.

Marshes, Bogs, and More

There are many types of wetlands, but the main ones are marshes, swamps, and bogs. The differences in each type depend on how long the area is wet each year, what kinds of plants grow there, and what kind of soil lies underneath. Some wetlands stretch along seacoasts, so they contain salt water. Others are inland and hold freshwater.

A bog looks like a meadow, but its soil is wet and spongy.

Wetlands come in all sizes, too. Some are only small ponds. Others are thousands of acres, like the Florida Everglades.

Marshes, which usually contain freshwater, sometimes lie along the edges of rivers and lakes. They may be wet all year or only part of the year. Many types of grasses grow in marshes. And they provide habitat for many small water animals, such as crayfish, snails, and frogs. Larger mammals, such as raccoons and deer, need marshes for drinking and fishing. Of course, birds, especially waterbirds like ducks, raise their young in marshes. There is plenty of food and tall grasses for shelter.

Ducks nest and raise their young in wetlands.

This swamp near the Everglades in Florida is full of large cypress trees.

Swamps are not always wet year-round, but they hold water most of the year. A big difference between marshes and swamps is that many trees and shrubs grow in swamps. These woody plants spread out their shallow roots under the mud that forms when rivers flood in spring or during heavy storms.

Bogs differ from both marshes and swamps because they don't get their water from rivers, lakes, or oceans. The water in bogs comes only from rainfall, so bogs usually are found where there are heavy rains throughout most of the year. The main plants in bogs are mosses and several

This black bear is passing through a Pennsylvania bog.

types of berries, such as cranberries and blueberries. Only a few animals, such as turtles, otters, and mink, live in bogs.

Clearly, wetlands are very important for the survival of wildlife. But wetlands do more than provide a habitat for plants and animals. People also are helped by wetlands, though many of us don't realize it.

Wonderful Wetlands

Wetlands help control flooding. They act like sponges, holding extra water when the snow melts each spring, and after heavy rains. However, when wetlands are destroyed and replaced by concrete or houses, the extra water has nowhere to go. So, it overfills streams and rivers, flooding towns and farm fields. Homes can be ruined, and farmers may be unable to plant or harvest their crops.

Wetlands located along waterways act like sponges, soaking up water during heavy storms or when snow melts.

Wetlands help farmers by keeping groundwater pure. They filter out sediments and harmful chemicals. They can hold water and reduce flooding. During dry years, grass often continues to grow around wetlands, providing food for cattle and attracting wildlife.

Wetlands are also a natural way of treating some of the less toxic pollutants in runoff, such as fertilizers from lawns and manure from animals.

Wetlands also can treat wastewater that goes down drains after it has been used by people or businesses. This water often carries with it a variety of chemicals. Expensive wastewater-treatment plants clean the water and make it pure again. But wetlands do this naturally. It is a less costly method and works just as well.

Animals such as oysters and shrimp live and raise their young in coastal wetlands.

Wetlands clean most pollutants from water. The chemicals slowly settle to the bottom. There, they are trapped in mud. Pesticides are broken down by marsh plants into harmless substances, or trapped in the sediment filtered from the water. Many towns with serious water-pollution problems in lakes and rivers have found that improving their wetlands helps clean up the pollution.

Wetlands are also an important source of food. They provide a home for such animals as fish, shrimp, ducks, and oysters. Many people also enjoy the berries from bogs. In some parts of the world people heat their homes with a fuel called peat, which is produced in bogs.

Golfing on a Swamp

However, in spite of their benefits, thousands of acres of wetlands are being destroyed each year. Many people do not understand and appreciate wetlands. They think wetlands are useless wasteland, so the people cover them over and fill them in with soil. Or they drain the water out of them to create dry land. They build golf courses, parking lots, homes, and businesses on them, or they use them for growing crops. This has been going on for hundreds of years.

Most wetlands in North America have been lost by being turned into farmland. About 25 percent of the farmland in Canada and the United States was once wetland.

Today in the United States, a law says people must get special permission before they destroy any wetland, even if it is on property they own. And usually, for every piece of wetland they cover, the law suggests they build an equal amount of wetland somewhere else.

When a highway was being built in Wisconsin, a wetland was destroyed. The law required the state to build another wetland to replace the one that was lost.

Protecting Wetlands

Most of the wetlands lost throughout the United States were filled in for farmland. Now, the federal government is helping farmers restore the wetlands.

The Wetlands Reserve Program offers farmers and other landowners money if they restore and protect wetlands on their property. The U.S. Department of Agriculture expects to have one million acres (404,000 hectares) of wetlands in this program by 1995.

Many landowners are happy to join the program—and not only for the money. Farmland that was once wetland often is too moist to grow healthy plants.

To participate in the Wetlands Reserve Program, landowners must sign an agreement to restore and protect wetlands on their property. They still may be able to use the land for such activities as hunting, fishing, cutting timber, and grazing, but each piece of property is different. No activities that will damage the wetlands are allowed.

When the property is sold, the future owners must agree to care for the wetlands. In this way, wetlands will be preserved for generations to come.

Mother Nature Knows Best

Building a wetland may sound like a good idea, but unfortunately, it is a very difficult task for human beings. People can prepare the ground. They can put in a selection of the right kind of plants. But the wetlands they build are never as good as those created by nature. Nature always manages to get just the right mix of plants together in just the right locations. And nature attracts the right wildlife to use the wetlands. People may not always be as successful.

And even with the recent laws, as much as 500,000 acres of wetlands—800 square miles (202,000 hectares)—are lost every year. About half of the 200 million acres (81 million hectares) of

These men are building a wetland where a strip mine used to be located.

wetlands that once existed in the United States are gone. Many remaining wetlands are being ruined by pollution.

Concern over Chemicals

Pollution from animal waste can be stopped if farmers are careful.

When harmful chemicals get into water that goes through a wetland, some fish, plants, and animals can no longer live in the polluted wetlands. The water cannot be used as drinking water for people, either. It is not healthy even to swim in the lakes or rivers that lie nearby.

Pollution often comes from places in the town where sewage from toilets and sinks is treated. It also comes from factories that dump wastewater containing chemicals directly into water sources. The sources of such pollution can be located.

It is not possible, however, to say exactly where other kinds of pollution come from, though we have a general knowledge. Most of it consists of chemicals that the rain washes off city streets, farm fields, and construction sites. The rainwater carries this runoff into natural waterways. Because it comes from many sources and enters the waterways at many points, this general pollution is very difficult to control.

runoff = water that flows off land into waterways, often carrying pollution with it.

In the United States, the Clean Water Act requires all states to investigate and control water pollution. It also provides funding for some solutions, such as processing the runoff from storm sewers. Cities and towns can learn to manage land better to prevent runoff and erosion. Farmers can learn how to prevent erosion and use fewer chemicals on their fields. All these things will help.

The Clean Water Act also aims to prevent pollution from known sources. Strict laws limit the amount of waste that cities and factories can discharge into waterways. Offenders are heavily fined and must clean up the damage.

Undoing the Damage

Fortunately, most wetlands have the natural ability to repair themselves once people make some effort to clean them up and keep them healthy. But more people need to become aware of

This visitors' center is built over Kingland Creek Marsh in the Hackensack River of New Jersey next to an area where garbage used to be dumped. This area is being transformed into a park built of several hundred acres of reclaimed dumps and wetlands.

the damage being done. Those who break the laws should be punished severely, and cleanup work must continue.

Many projects have been set up to repair, restore, and replace wetlands. Some are like the Wetlands Conservancy, which is preserving wetlands in Oregon. Other states have similar programs, and many of the most successful projects are being done by communities.

In Maryland, a lake's shoreline was being eroded. Usually, man-made structures, such as concrete walls, are used to hold the soil in place. But one community planted marsh grasses and other water-loving plants. These plants send their roots down into the soil and hold it in place. Not only do they look more attractive than concrete, but they

People in a group called Environmental Concern planted marsh grasses along a Maryland lake to hold the soil in place (right). The photo above shows the same shoreline several months after the grasses were planted (above).

are less expensive, require less care, and do the job just as well. Much of the planting is done by handicapped adults, who get satisfaction and pride from helping the environment.

Building a Bog—Making a Marsh

Two basic types of wetlands can be made by people. Some are called "constructed" wetlands. Others are "created" wetlands. The two terms are similar, but they mean different things.

Constructed wetlands are made to clean wastewater and improve water quality. They can be fairly simple and still get the job done.

Created wetlands, on the other hand, are made mainly to benefit nature by providing homes for the plants and animals that will live there. They are more difficult for people to make.

Usually an industry or a local government builds a constructed wetland to handle its wastewater. Sometimes homeowners in rural areas will build one. These wetlands handle sewage, runoff from mines and farms, and other types of pollutants. The polluted liquid is allowed to run downhill into the wetland. The plants and mud absorb the pollution. Then the water—cleaned of its pollutants—enters the lake or other waterway.

Some homes have their own small wetlands for wastewater treatment.

Constructed wetlands are made up of different ponds that contain plants and animals that clean wastewater.

Since constructed wetlands have so many uses, they come in many forms. Some are small gravel beds with only a few plants. Others are large habitats for a wide variety of plants and animals.

Constructed wetlands are a low-cost way to remove pollutants from wastewater. But they don't always work perfectly. Much depends upon the time of year and how much water the wetland holds.

Another problem occurs when the wetlands have absorbed too many chemicals. These chemicals may be harmful to the animals that come to live there. They can cause illness and even death. And sometimes, too, chemicals trapped by wetlands seep into the groundwater. This can be dangerous to the many people who get their drinking water from groundwater.

Created wetlands usually are built by people who want to help the environment. Also, according to the law, builders who destroy a wetland area must create another one somewhere else. Creating wetlands to meet the needs of wildlife is a fairly new idea, so people aren't sure exactly how to do it. They rarely do as good a job as nature does on its own. Usually, there are fewer types of plants growing in created wetlands, and fewer animals living in them. Much more research and practice are needed as people try to improve created wetlands.

The great blue heron is a water-bird that lives in wetlands.

Different Plans for Different Places

When people build wetlands, they must do it differently each time. That's because the surrounding areas always are different. Sometimes there is already a great deal of water. Abandoned gravel

This old rock quarry is being reclaimed as a beautiful wetland.

Large earth moving equipment is used to build ponds for a new wetland.

This engineer is testing the water quality in a constructed wetland to be sure it is clean and safe.

pits, for example, often are so deep that groundwater seeps into them. They also collect rainwater. Gravel and rocks may be dumped into the pits to make them shallower.

Other times, there may be a pond that is too shallow for a wetland. People must make it deep enough to reach down into the groundwater. The groundwater can then fill it.

Sometimes, people want to build a wetland such as a bog in a place where there is no groundwater. In that case, they have to dig a pond and line it with clay or heavy rubber. The clay or rubber won't let water seep into the soil. These wetlands are built in a low spot so that rainwater can drain into them from all around.

The best soil for filling in a wetland is soil from a nearby wetland. This soil probably will contain seeds, small plants, and tiny insects that will live and grow in the new wetland. It's also a good idea to take larger plants and grasses from a nearby wetland, and plant them next to the new wetland.

Next—the wetland builders hope—come the animals. With a little help from people, nature takes care of this part pretty well. Many waterbirds and mammals come quite easily. They are attracted by the water. Many insects that like wetlands, such as dragonflies, arrive rather quickly, too. Other small water creatures, such as leeches and snails, usually come along with the soil and plants taken from nearby wetlands. Waterbirds also carry these small creatures in on their legs. Gradually, the wetland becomes almost like a natural one.

Insects such as dragonflies lay their eggs and live in wetlands.

Worldwide Wetland Work

Wetlands are being created throughout the world. In Great Britain, for example, there is a strong push to create more wetlands in urban areas. Wetlands are quite important to the country's wildlife. Thousands of ducks, geese, and swans rest each autumn in Britain's wetlands as they migrate southward. The birds travel from the chilly regions of Greenland, Scandinavia, and

This park in urban Tokyo has a wetland and beautiful greenery giving people a place to relax.

Russia, to the warmer air of southern Africa. They stop again in spring as they fly north. Without wetlands, the birds won't come.

Many people are finally realizing how important wetlands are. They are learning how to build new ones. But more importantly, they are working to preserve the remaining wetlands. It is not too late to keep our wetlands healthy if we all work together.

Cattail Cleaners

Cattails fill the wetland near the American Electric Power Plant in Conesville, Ohio. This healthy wetland is expanding, providing all the benefits to the area that any wetland does. But this wetland does something else, too.

It is a constructed wetland, made especially to treat polluted water in the area. The water is polluted because it flows through an abandoned underground and surface mine site. On its way, the water picks up iron that can be harmful to people, animals, and most plants.

However, researchers have found that cattails and several other wetland plants grow especially well in water containing iron. As these plants grow, they pull iron from the water to help them grow. When the water leaves the wetland, most of the iron has been removed. Many other harmful chemicals have been filtered out, too.

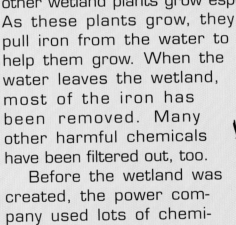

Before the wetland was created, the power company used lots of chemicals to help flush out the iron and purify the water. Now, hardly any chemicals are used at all. The wetland does the job naturally and safely.

Cities Cover the Land

Every day, cities around the world are getting bigger. Each person born will need a place on the Earth to live. Some will drive cars that need roads built over the land. All will produce waste that must go somewhere.

Taking care of these needs uses resources from the land, causing problems. People certainly do create many of the problems faced by the Earth and its soil. But people can create solutions, too.

A simple example is garbage. Did you ever think about what happens to the trash you throw away? And what about the garbage from all the other people in the nation?

Orlando, Florida (above), is growing very rapidly. Buildings, roads, and parking lots are covering the land.

Burying Our Problems

The trash you put in your household trash cans is taken away by a big truck. It is put with all the trash from the homes and businesses in your town.

Trash used to be taken to open pits, or garbage dumps. Today, the dumps have been turned into special pits called landfills. These landfills are big holes carved out of the ground. They are lined with special material to keep dangerous chemicals from soaking into the soil and groundwater. As garbage is dumped on top, big machines crush it into as small a space as possible. Each day, a layer of soil is spread over the garbage. When the landfill is full, more soil is placed over it. Sometimes grass and trees are planted on top.

landfill = a specially prepared place where waste is dumped and covered by layers of soil.

Truckloads of dirt are moved when a landfill is built.

One problem with landfills is that many liners leak over time. Then chemicals can get into the soil—and even into the groundwater. To keep this from happening, many landfills won't accept cars, batteries, or appliances that contain dangerous chemicals. They won't accept cleaning fluids, motor oil, or paint, either. Homeowners have to find other ways to dispose of these chemicals rather than dumping them in their garbage.

Clean Sweep

Some communities have a "Clean Sweep Day" once or twice a year. People bring their harmful chemicals to a special location, where experts collect and properly dispose of them. Paint, varnish, harsh cleaning liquids, and pesticides are among the items that must be handled separately from regular trash.

Many gas stations have a special container just for used motor oil. Oil should always be taken to a station rather than just thrown away. And stores that sell large car batteries will recycle the old ones their customers bring in. It is important to our land and water that such items be disposed of safely.

Special landfills with extra-thick liners have been built in some cities. These landfills can hold dangerous chemicals more safely. Still, these liners may leak someday. It's better to avoid using chemicals that cause problems in the first place.

Landfills are huge areas near our cities filled with garbage. And they are ugly. But people who manage landfills are trying to clean up their act.

Usually, once a landfill is as high as it should go, it is covered with soil. Grass, shrubs, and trees are planted on it. Sometimes, covered landfills are used for playgrounds and golf courses.

recycling = converting used, scrap, or waste material into new products. This is the symbol for recycling.

On Clean Sweep Days volunteers collect harmful chemicals and other trash.

Three Ps Against Pollution

Nearly 20 years ago, the 3M Company in Minnesota started its 3P Program, which stands for "Pollution Prevention Pays." Every employee at all of 3M's plants helps. They try to find new, creative ways to reduce, re-use, or recycle the chemicals they are using. They want to find better, safer methods.

The 3P Program has worked out very well. For example, when 3M makes videotapes, a great deal of waste is created in the process. This waste is a chemical called aluminum sulfate. The company used to just throw the waste away, but it now sells the waste to fertilizer factories. These factories turn the aluminum sulfate into plant food. The chemical is re-used safely and 3M makes money, too.

The workers in the picture are making a liquid absorbent for industry. This product is made out of material trimmed off when face masks are made. The company used to throw this waste away. Now it is recycled into a useful product.

Many times, 3M's new ways are cheaper than the old methods. 3M has cut its wastes by nearly half, and saved over $350 million.

Too Much Trash

The biggest problem with landfills is that they cost so much and the world is running out of places to put them. It is much better to use good land for agriculture, or to save it for wilderness, than to fill it with garbage. But until we reduce the amount of garbage we produce, we'll have to find somewhere to put it.

The United States alone produces more than 11 billion tons (10 billion metric tons) of waste each year. There are currently about 6,000 landfills in the country. But one-third of these will have to close soon because they are full.

Many people think that garbage in landfills will decompose, breaking down into tiny pieces that become part of the soil. A great deal of garbage does decompose, but it takes a long time for this to happen.

It takes cardboard milk cartons (above) five years to decompose in a landfill. These hot dogs (below) were in a landfill for ten years without decomposing.

Milk cartons take about five years to decompose, according to the Quality of Life Committee in Madisonville, Tennessee. Plastic bags take 10 to 20 years, and plastic containers won't decompose for at least 50 to 80 years.

Orange peels are quicker. They take about half a year to decompose, and paper takes a little bit less than that. But aluminum cans, such as those that soda comes in, need at least 90 years to decompose. And plastic foam, like Styrofoam cups, will *never* decompose.

Rave about Recycling

The best solution is to create less garbage, so we won't need as many landfills. Recycling cans, plastic and glass containers, newspapers, and other waste is something we all can do. In addition to saving land, recycling keeps other land from becoming new mine sites and landfills.

We also can re-use things. Instead of throwing away an old flannel shirt, you could cut it up into cleaning rags. Then you wouldn't need paper towels for cleaning. We can repair items when they break or take them to places such as Goodwill Industries so they can be re-used. Also, we can reduce future garbage by purchasing fewer items.

Composting is another idea. People can collect their grass clippings and other yard waste in a heap. They can add things like fruit and vegetable leftovers—but no meat. They also can add animal manure, because it contains special nutrients. They leave the whole pile for a while, turning it occasionally. Gradually it decomposes into good humus for the soil. It can be mixed with regular soil to add nutrients.

composting = a process in which natural materials such as leaves, grass, and food remains decompose and turn into a material known as humus. It is rich in nutrients and can be added to the soil.

When compost is added to soil, it makes the soil loose and adds nutrients.

Recycled Asphalt Pavement

No city in the United States has more miles of roads than Los Angeles, California. Keeping these roads in good shape is hard work, and it can produce a great deal of waste.

When a new surface, or pavement, was put on roads, the old pavement used to be thrown away. This was not only a terrible waste, but it also added to the trash being dumped in landfills.

Now a new program has been started. The City of Los Angeles's Bureau of Street Maintenance is using recycled asphalt pavement (called RAP) to resurface roads. Asphalt is made from gravel or sand mixed with thick petroleum products. Old asphalt pavement from cracked and broken streets is crushed. When the crushed asphalt is heated, it can be used again for street repair. Up to 1,200 tons (1,090 metric tons) of old asphalt are processed this way each day in the city. There are no hazards to the environment.

By 1994, more than 800,000 tons (726,000 metric tons) of asphalt had been recycled. Los Angeles has saved more than $8 million as well as valuable landfill space. In addition, less petroleum has to be used to make new asphalt pavement. This is a good way to recycle wastes and help the environment.

New Trends for Trash

Many communities also are looking at other ways to cut down on garbage. Some use garbage as fuel. They burn it to help create electricity in power plants. A company called Oxford Energy, for example, has a plant near Modesto, California, that burns old rubber tires. It uses about five million tires each year, and makes enough electricity for 14,000 nearby homes.

In other towns, all types of garbage are burned to create energy. About one-tenth of the garbage in the United States is handled this way. This may sound like a good solution for getting rid of trash, but trash-burning is expensive and can create air pollution. Power plants must first spend a huge amount of money to build devices that keep pollution out of the air. But some material still escapes. Also, a great deal of ash is left over after the burning, and it goes into landfills.

The Oxford Energy Company burns rubber tires instead of coal to produce electricity.

Many communities have their own recycling programs, too. The landfills in Newark, New Jersey, were all filled up in 1987. The city quickly had to figure out something else to do with its garbage. Some of it was trucked to another state, but that was very expensive. So instead, Newark made plans to increase its recycling. This program is successful today. The city recycles more than half of its garbage, and even earns money by recycling. Scrap metal and old newspapers are sold to recycling companies.

Local businesses and citizens are taking part, too. Offices in Newark recycle 80 percent of their paper. Residents used to recycle 100 tons (91 metric tons) of trash each month. Now they recycle seven times as much—more waste than any other city on the East Coast of the United States.

We're Running Out of Room

But there are still more problems for the land. As the number of people on Earth increases, cities grow, too. All these new people need places to live, work, and drive. The space for living comes from land that was once used for farms, wetlands, prairies, or wilderness. Parking lots are built where corn once grew. Quiet river valleys are turned into industrial parks. Apartment buildings are constructed on wetlands that have been filled in.

In the United States since 1970, each year an average of over 1.3 million acres (500,000 hectares) have been developed into urban areas. About three million acres (1.2 million hectares) of farmland are taken over for other purposes each year, too.

Many greenbelts have bikeways for people of all ages to enjoy.

In order to keep some land open, more and more cities have created greenbelts. Greenbelts are large strips of land that are left to nature. They often connect parks and other natural areas. Some are completely within the city, and others are found between the city and suburbs. Greenbelts are good for animals, because they can travel through them—sort of like roads. People also like greenbelts. They can use them for hiking, biking, and horseback riding. They are nice to look at, too.

In the city of Chicago, Illinois, and its suburbs, there are more than 350 miles (560 kilometers) of greenbelts. People in the area hope there will be even more. Throughout the United States, more than two million acres (0.8 million hectares) of natural areas are being preserved in this way.

The people of Denver, Colorado, have changed an ugly warehouse area next to the river (right) into a beautiful green area of bikeways, trails, and parks (left).

Open spaces are like greenbelts. They are large patches of land left to nature. Some local communities have laws about open space. Many times, when apartments go up or factories and offices are built, the developer must keep some open space on the property. This helps to save homes for many plants and wild animals.

Paving Paradise

Even with greenbelts and open spaces, buildings cover more and more land today. So does pavement. In the United States alone, 60,000 square miles (155,000 square kilometers) of land are used for roads and parking lots. As much as 10 percent of the country's potential farmland is used for roads. And in Britain, more than 4,000 acres (1,600 hectares) of countryside are covered over each year for roads. Are there better ways to use this land?

These volunteers in Berkeley, California, are tearing up an old parking lot so they can plant a garden.

What would happen if no more roads were built? No more forests would be cut down to make room for roads. No more wetlands would be covered over. Birds and animals could stay in their homes. And we'd save lots of money and have less car pollution. But is that possible?

A group called the Alliance for a Paving Moratorium says yes. The group wants no more roads to be built or widened, and no more parking lots, either. Members say there are only two good reasons for putting more pavement on the land. These reasons are to repair roads we already have, and to build paths for walking and biking.

The group hopes that with no new roads, fewer people will want to drive cars. Right now in the United States, there are more than 140 million cars. Instead of driving, people could walk, ride a bike, or take a bus or train. This would help cut down on the air pollution caused by cars. It also would reduce the number of people killed each year in car accidents. And no more land would be spoiled by building a road on it.

Work Together for the Future

We must work to save our planet—to keep it sustainable for future generations. People must learn to work with nature. After all, we are all part of the Earth and its resources.

Everyone should be able to survive using these resources. But we must not use them up. The people who come after us will need Earth's resources, too. We have to learn to care for the land. At the United Nations Earth Summit in Brazil in 1992, every country made a commitment to create a sustainable future for itself and the Earth. Now it is up to each of us to do our part and work together to have a healthy, safe, and beautiful planet.

SURE! Growing Smart

In Richmond, Indiana, the Sustainable Urban/Rural Enterprise, known as SURE, works with many groups to make "sure" that Richmond's growth is good for the Earth. The city already has recycling and energy conservation programs.

It also is developing a natural greenbelt city park. SURE helps residents with such projects as community cleanups and neighborhood gardens.

In addition, SURE has carefully studied the land around Richmond. The information the members gather helps them decide where to best locate new parks, shopping malls, factories, and homes. They want to make sure that they are using the city's resources as wisely as possible.

But SURE doesn't work only within the city of Richmond. It also helps farmers in

the area learn about sustainable agriculture. Farmers are encouraged to sell some of their produce at city markets.

Many other communities are looking at the success SURE has had in Richmond. They want to do something similar. People are learning that they must plan cities to take care of the environment.

PLACES TO WRITE

You can get more information or find out what you can do to help by writing to one of these organizations:

American Farmland Trust
1920 N Street, NW, Suite 400
Washington, DC 20036

Canadian Nature Federation
1673 Carling Avenue
Ottawa, Ontario, Canada K2A 3Z1

Environmental Defense Fund
257 Park Avenue South
New York, NY 10010

Friends of the Earth
218 D Street, SE
Washington, DC 20003

National Audubon Society
6435 Pennsylvania Avenue, SE
Washington, DC 20003

International Alliance for
Sustainable Agriculture
1701 University Ave SE
Minneapolis, MN 55414

National Wildlife Federation
1412 16th Street, N.
Washington, DC 20036

The Nature Conservancy
1815 N. Lynn Street
Arlington, VA 22209

Worldwatch Institute
1776 Massachusetts Avenue, NW
Washington, DC 20036

GLOSSARY

composting – a process in which natural materials such as leaves, grass, and food remains decompose and turn into humus. It is rich in nutrients and can be added to the soil.

decompose – to break down into nutrients that can be re-used by plants and animals.

desertification – a process in which good, healthy land is turned into desert. Harmful farming practices may cause desertification.

developing countries – countries where the industry and the economy are not modern.

erosion – the wearing away of land surfaces by the action of wind or water.

excrement – the solid waste, or manure, given off by an animal after it digests it food.

fallow – unplanted.

fertile – having enough nutrients to grow crops.

fertilizer – a substance applied to soil to add nutrients.

groundwater – water that fills the spaces found in some rock formations beneath the Earth's surface. Groundwater is often used for drinking water by digging a well down into it.

humus – the richest part of soil containing nutrients from decomposed plant and animal matter.

landfill – a specially prepared place where waste is dumped and covered by layers of soil.

lichen – a combination of two plants—a one-celled plant called an alga and a fungus.

microorganism – an animal or plant, such as bacteria or fungus, that is so small it can be seen only with a microscope.

natural resource – a material found in or on the Earth that is useful to people.

nomads – people who herd animals and move from place to place to find pasture and good water. They have no fixed home, but depend on their animals for food.

nutrients – substances in food or fertilizers that allow plants and animals to live and grow.

pesticide – a chemical used to kill weeds, fungi, insects, or rodents.

pollution – any addition to land, water, or air that makes it dirty or unusable.

reclamation – the process of repairing damaged land, so that it can be used for farmland, recreation, or other useful purposes.

recycling – converting used, scrap, or waste material into new products.

runoff – water that runs off land into waterways, often carrying pollution with it.

sediment – soil, sand, or other matter that settle on the ground after being carried away by wind or water.

sustainable agriculture – growing enough healthy food for everyone in a way that won't hurt the Earth or its people.

tailings – the waste material left after a mineral is separated from rock.

tilling – plowing the land to prepare it for raising crops.

topsoil – the surface layer of soil in which most of the nutrients are found.

wastewater – water that has been used by homes or businesses.

wetlands – lands that are flooded part or all of the year. Many plants and animals live in wetlands.

INDEX

ABOUT THE AUTHOR

Terri Willis, a former newspaper reporter, is the author of several books and articles on the environment. Her books include *Cars: The Environmental Challenge*, co-written with Wallace B. Black, and *Land Use and Abuse*, both from the SAVING PLANET EARTH series. She has contributed three books to the WONDERS OF THE WORLD series: *St. Lawrence River and Seaway*, *Serengeti Plain*, and *Sichuan Forests of the Panda*. A graduate of the University of Wisconsin at Madison, Terri lives in Lake Geneva, Wisconsin, with her husband, Harry, and her two daughters, Andrea and Elizabeth.